Hawai'i One Summer

Lone tree along the coast.
Lāna'i, Hawai'i.

Maxine Hong Kingston

Hawai'i One Summer

A Latitude 20 Book

University of Hawai'i Press
Honolulu

First published in the United States in 1987 by Meadow Press, San Francisco. Published in 1998 by University of Hawai'i Press.

With the exception of the two Prefaces and "Lew Welch: An Appreciation," these ten pieces appeared in *The New York Times* in 1978, all, except "A Sea Worry," as a weekly column entitled "Hers," and are published here with the permission of *The New York Times* and Alfred A. Knopf, Inc.

Quotes from the poetry of Lew Welch are from *Ring of Bone, Collected Poems 1950–1971* © 1973 Grey Fox Press, with acknowledgment to Donald Allen.

Photographs © 1998 by Franco Salmoiraghi

Printed in the United States of America

03 02 01 00 99 98   5 4 3 2 1

Library of Congress Cataloging-in-Publication Data
Kingston, Maxine Hong.
  Hawai'i one summer / Maxine Hong Kingston.
    p.   cm.
  "A Latitude 20 book."
  Originally published: San Francisco : Meadow Press, 1987.
  ISBN 0–8248–1887–3 (pbk.)
  1. Kingston, Maxine Hong—Homes and haunts—Hawaii.   2. Women authors, American—20th century—Biography.   3. Women authors, American—Hawaii—Biography.   4. Chinese Americans—Hawaii—Biography.   5. Hawaii—Social life and customs.   6. Hawaii—Civilization.   I. Title.
PS3561.I52Z468   1998
818'.5403—dc21
                                                    98–21407
                                                       CIP

University of Hawai'i Press books are printed on acid-free paper and meet the guidelines for permanence and durability of the Council on Library Resources *to the friends who are in this book*

Contents

Preface to the Paperback Edition

I wrote these essays during the middle of our seventeen-year
stay in Hawai'i. Reading them today, I see that I have
changed, and Hawai'i has changed. I am happier, and
Hawai'i is more wonderful. A black cloud had covered my home
place, Northern California. But leaving the Mainland for Hawai'i
had not gotten us out from under it. The black pall that spread
over the world during the long war had still not lifted. In 1978, the
year of the Summer of this book, I was continuing my depression
from the Vietnam War. The fallout from that war went on and on
—wars in Cambodia and Laos, MIAs, agent orange, boat people.

A reader of this book surprises me. She asks, Why the many
allusions to suicide? I reread these pages, and see: *Mortgage*
meant *death*. The bombing of Kaho'olawe—by ANZUS and
Japan. My son haunted by the ghosts of Mānoa, and I haunted by
the ghost of a lost poet. Nature's creatures suffering and killing.
Kālua pig looking like a haole human being. And homesickness
—but if I do not feel at home in Paradise, where is home? My
first take on Hawai'i was, Here I am arrived at the Land of Lotus
Eaters, and I'm not going to leave. I thought I was writing light-
hearted essays.

This same sympathetic reader wondered, Could it be that
you'd broken taboos by writing and publishing secrets? Well, it
did not feel good to be a writer in a place that is not a writing
culture, where written language is only a few hundred years old.
The literary community in Hawai'i argues over who owns the
myths and stories, whether the local language and writings should

be exported to the Mainland, whether or not so-and-so is
authentic, is Hawai'i. For me, Hawai'i was a good place for
writing about California and China, and not for writing about
Hawai'i. I felt the kapu—these are not your stories to write; these
myths are not your myths; the Hawaiians are not your people.
You are haole. You are katonk. My great grandfathers, one on my
mother's side, one on my father's side, and my paternal grand-
father lived and worked in Hawai'i. Even so, they were not
kama'āina, and I am not kama'āina.

Once, on the Big Island, Pele struck me blind. She didn't want
me to look at her, nor to write about her. I could hear her say,
"So you call yourself Woman Warrior, do you? Take that." I feel
fear even now as I write her name. And I could hear the
Hawaiians: "You have taken our land. Don't take our stories."

Hawai'i held an Asian Pacific American writers' conference
the very Summer of this book. We addressed one another with
rancor and panic, though some did try for aloha. The name *Asian
Pacific American* had barely been thought, and many people
denied every term in it. We were divided between those who
would give the stories, myths, ceremonies to whoever hears them,
and those who would have possession be by blood. So, I decided
that I would write personally, about myself and my family, about
homesickness for California, and my upcoming high school
reunion, about washing the dishes, teaching school, reading. I
would publish these humble pieces in New York, and bypass
Hawai'i. I meant to honor kapu, not touch kapu things at all.

But though I did try to leave her out, Hawai'i—people sing
her and speak of her as Spirit—made her way into these essays.
Writing about buying our first house, I worried that I was trying
to own property that had been a Royal Hawaiian Land Grant.
Describing Nature, the sea, the air, the lands and fish, is
describing Hawai'i. I studied Lew Welch on dialect because
I was thinking about Hawai'i's language—how to teach standard
English to students who speak pidgin without offending or
harming them?

Now, a dozen years after leaving her, I realize a way free to
tell a story of Hawai'i.

In 1980, I was recognized as a Living Treasure of Hawai'i.
The enrobed monks and priests of the Honpa Hongwanji Mission
at the temple on the Pali chanted Sanskrit, and passed a certificate
through the incense that entitles me to "all the rights, privileges,
and consideration" of a Living Treasure of Hawai'i. Some of my
fellow Living Treasures are Mary Kawena Pukui, Gabby Pahinui,
Herb Kawainui Kane, Francis Haar, Bumpei Akaji, Satoru Abe,
Auntie Irmgard Farden Aluli, Don Mitchell, Auntie Emma
Farden Sharp, Tadashi Sato, Eddie Kamai, and everybody, really,
only not yet formally recognized in ceremony.

As a responsible Living Treasure, I feel called upon to tell
you a story that will give help and power. Once there was a
prophecy that Kamehameha would conquer all the islands if he
could build a great temple to his family war god, Kū-kā'ili-moku.
Setting some of the lava rocks and boulders with his own hands,

Kamehameha built the heiau on Puʻukoholā, the Hill of the
Whale, at Kawaihae. His domain at that time was the northwest
half of the Big Island. Before the heiau could be finished, the
chiefs of Maui, Lānaʻi, Molokaʻi, Kauaʻi, and Oʻahu raised
an armada and attacked Kamehameha's land and people.
Kamehameha repelled the attack, and completed the building of
the massive temple. To dedicate it, he summoned his cousin,
Keoua Kūʻahuʻula, ruler of the rest of the Big Island, to come to
the ceremony. It was understood that Keoua Kūʻahuʻula would be
the gift to the war god. In honor, he could not refuse this call, but
he emasculated himself; Kamehameha would not have a perfect
male sacrifice. Kamehameha waiting on shore, Keoua Kūʻahuʻula
arose in his canoe. Kamehameha's counselor and father-in-law,
Keʻeaumoku, killed him. Keoua's blood and body sanctified the
new temple. Enmity between their two clans lasted for two
hundred years.

In 1991, descendants of Kamehameha and descendants of
Keoua Kūʻahuʻula had an inspiration "to heal the bitterness,
grievances, and enmity of the past two hundred years." The families gathered at Puʻukoholā Heiau, and re-created the event of
long ago: Keoua Kūʻahuʻula approaches Kamehameha. This
time, they meet and walk on together.

To Kamehameha I, unification meant conquering all the
Hawaiian people by war. Now unification is the coming together
of former enemies in peace. It is possible to heal history. It is
possible to be one people living in harmony.

I heard the above story from Jim Houston, who heard it from
the Park Service and from Kalani Meinecke, who narrated the
unification ceremony at Puʻukoholā Heiau.

I am not the person I was in the "War" essay, and the "Dishwashing" essay. Now looking back at Sanctuary at the Church of
the Crossroads, I remember the AWOL soldiers who were true
pacifist heroes. And the black cloud no longer hangs over
Hawaiʻi. I am more joyful and hopeful than when I was young.
And I love washing dishes, which attitude is the answer to *that*
koan.

Ke aloha nō! Aloha!

Mainland, 1998

P.S. I must tell you about the incarnations of the pieces in this
book. Most of them first appeared in my "Hers" column in the
New York Times, which rejected "Lew Welch: An Appreciation."
I thought: New York is too provincial to understand the Pacific
Rim. But now I see that I didn't follow Lew Welch's disappear-
ance far enough. He got off at *leina-a-ka-ʻuhane,* leaping place of
souls. I owe this poetic insight to Victoria Nelson of *My Time in
Hawaii;* our times coincided.

Leigh McLellan of Meadow Press gathered these pieces, and
made a book of them with her own loving hands. She chose paper
from the Kozo rice fields in Korea, hand-set the type, made the
paste paper for the cover, and sewed the binding. The Taoist
teacher, Deng Ming-Dao, son of Jade Snow Wong, cut and

printed four beautiful six-color woodblock pictures. There are
150 books, half of them in clipcases that Leigh constructed. It is
a luxury to hold and touch and smell one of these books. But, at
$400 per book and $500 for the slipcased one, the fine print
edition of *Hawai'i One Summer* is for art collectors, and not
for readers.

So, these writings, once ephemeral newspaper articles, then
revered artifacts, have found their just-right form—the paperback
in your hand.

Preface

wenty years after an adventure, I can write about it truly. A few large shapes remain in the memory—unforgettable. A thing which at one time seemed monumental becomes background or a surprisingly small figure in front, or it has disappeared. Remember how stereopticon pictures look like popping 3-D with cut-out-like cars and buildings and people artificially forward and backward? Memory is artistic in the ways it arranges and sorts out. My son is exactly twenty years old, and what I remember of his being born was a big hand holding a little foot. I am forty-three years old, and I just noticed that the hero in the novel I'm working on is twenty-three. At last, I understand about being a young person setting out in the world.

I did not wait for twenty years to write the pieces in this book, which is like a diary. There is sometimes only a week or two between an event and my writing about it. I wrote about my son's surfing upon coming home from it. I wrote about the high school reunion before going to it. The result is that I am making up meanings as I go along. Which is the way I live anyway. There is a lot of detailed doubting here.

Since the invitation to the twentieth year high school reunion came at the beginning of the summer, I could have followed up and told you what happened next. But by August my worrying was all taken up by my son's surfing. Also, the reunion was so complicated—the people were so complicated—my seeing the child and the aging adult in others and in myself—that I have to wait until I'm still older to figure it out.

What I like very much about being middle-aged is that I can write from opposing points of view at once—rebel's and house-holder's, student's and teacher's, mother's and child's.

I was finishing *China Men* in the summer when other people were vacationing. So, for breaks, I wrote these pieces. But I was in the world of *China Men,* and its images kept appearing every-where—in my letters to friends, in life, and in this book. So, here again are the frigate birds in the air currents, creatures on the beach, assembly lines funneling napalm to Vietnam, the sandal-wood that was still here in Hawai'i when my great-grandfathers came.

It is very difficult to capture Hawai'i. Whose point of view among all of Hawai'i's peoples is the right way of seeing? Her beauty defies artistic imitation. There should be epic poems to her, as there were in ancient times. Failing that, I have instead and incidentally described her piece by piece, and hope that the sum praises her.

As I read over these essays, there is some grammar that I was tempted to clean up. I used to have a habit of saying "like," as in "like cool, man" and "like wow." It was my tribute to the slang of my generation. The twenty-three-year-old hero of my novel, which is set in Chinatown and North Beach in 1963, talks like that, and his style is spilling over into mine. Let it stand.

April 1984

Bed in Agee House.
Mānoa Valley, Honolulu.

Our First House

I t has been a month now since we moved into our own bought house. So far, we've been renters. I have liked saying, "Gotta make the rent" and "This much set aside for rent" and "rent party."

A renter can move quickly, no leases, forego the cleaning deposit and go. Plumbing, wiring, walls, roof, floors keep to their proper neutral places under the sun among the stars. If we looked at each other one day and decided that we really shouldn't have gotten married after all, we could dismantle the brick-and-plank bookshelf or leave it, no petty talk about material things. The householder is only one incarnation away from snail or turtle or kangaroo. In religions, the householder doesn't levitate like the monk. In politics, the householder doesn't say, "Burn it down to the ground." I had never become a housewife. I didn't need to own land to belong on this planet.

But as soon as we drove up to this house in Mānoa, we liked everything—the cascades of rosewood vines, lichen and moss on lava rock boulders, moss-color finches, two murky ponds thick with water hyacinth, an iridescent green toad—poisonous— hopping into the blue ginger, a gigantic monkey pod tree with a stone bench beneath it, three trees like Van Gogh's cypresses in the front yard, pines in back, an archway like an ear or an elbow with no purpose but to be walked through, a New England-type vestibule for taking off snowy coats and boots, a dining room with glass doors, only one bedroom but two makeshifts, a bath- room like a chapel, a kitchen with a cooler—through the slats you

can look down at the earth and smell it. And—the clincher—a
writer's garret, the very writer's garret of your imagination,
bookshelves along an entire wall and a window overlooking
plumeria in bloom and the ponds. If I could see through the
foliage, I could look downhill and see the (restored) hut where
Robert Louis Stevenson wrote his Hawai'i works.

What thick novels I could brood up here with no interrupting
chapter breaks but one long thought from front to back cover.

We found two concealed cupboards, one of them with seven
pigeonholes; the artist who painted in the garret must have stored
brushes in them, or perhaps, here, a sea captain or his widow kept
his rolled-up maps. The person who once sat at the built-in desk
(with a formica top) had written in pencil on the wall:

eros

agape

philos

Promising words.

But when we talked about house-buying, both of us thought
about dying. The brain automatically adds 20 years of mortgage
on to one's age. And *mortgage* derives from *mors, mortis,* as
in *mortal. Move* was one of the first English words my parents
ever used, such an early word I thought it was Chinese—
moo-fu, a Chinese American word that connotes "pick up your
pants and go."

Renting had begun to feel irresponsible. Our friend who
teaches university students how to calculate how many grams are

gained or lost on a protein exchange, how much alfalfa turns into how much hamburger, for example, told us about the time when each earthling will have one square foot of room. This friend quit the city and bought five acres in the mountains; a stream runs through his land. He will install solar energy panels and grow food, raise a goat, make the five acres a self-sufficient system.

We heard about a family who had all their teeth pulled, bought their own boat, and sailed for an island that's not on maps. If we owned a vacant lot somewhere, when the world ends, we can go there to sleep or sit.

Coincidentally, strange ads were appearing in the real estate section of newspapers: "Ideal place for you and your family in the event of war, famine, strike, or natural disaster."

The advantages—to have a place for meeting when the bombs fall and to write in a garret—outweighed the dread of ownership, and we bought the house.

The writer's garret is a myth about cheap housing. In real life, to have a garret, the writer has to own the house under the garret and the land under the house and the trees on the land for an inspiring view.

On the day we moved in, I tried walking about and thinking: "This is my tree. This flower is mine. This grass and dirt are mine." And they did partly belong to me.

Our son, Joseph, looked up at Tantalus, the mountain which rises straight up in back of the house, and said, "Do we have to rake up all the leaves that fall from there?"

At the escrow office (new word, *escrow*), we signed whatever
papers they told us to. Earll read them after we got home, and so
found out that this land had been given to E. H. Rogers by a Royal
Hawaiian Land Grant. "We don't belong on it," he said. But, I
rationalized, isn't all land Israel? No matter what year you claim
it, the property belongs to a former owner who has good moral
reason for a claim. Do we, for example, have a right to go to
China, and say we own our farm, which has belonged to our
family since 1100 A.D.? Ridiculous, isn't it? Also, doesn't the
average American move every five years? We just keep
exchanging with one another.

The way to deal with moving in was to establish a headquarters, which I decided would be in the dining room, a small
powerful spot, surprisingly not the garret, which is secretive.
The Headquarters would consist of a card table and a lawn chair,
a typewriter, papers, and pencils. It takes about ten minutes to set
up, and I feel moved in, capable; from the Headquarters, I will
venture into the rest of the house.

Earll assembles and talks about a Basic Kit, by which I think
he means a toothbrush and toothpaste. "The Basic Kit is all I
really need," he keeps saying, at which I take offense. I retaliate
that all I need is my Headquarters.

Joseph's method of moving in is to decide that his bedroom
will be the one in the attic, next to the writer's garret, and he
spreads everything he owns over its strangeness.

As at every place we have ever moved to, we throw mattresses on the living room floor and sleep there for several nights—to establish ourselves in the middle of the house, to weight it down. The night comes black into the uncurtained windows.

I attack the house from my Headquarters, and again appreciate being married to a person whose sense of geometry is not much different from mine. How do people stay together whose eyes can't agree on how much space there should be between pictures?

The final thing that makes it possible to live in the house is our promise to each other that if we cannot bear the weight of ownership, we can always sell, though we know from fifteen years of marriage that this is like saying, "Well, if this marriage doesn't work out, we can always get a divorce." You don't know how you change in the interim.

My High School Reunion

I just opened an envelope in the mail and found a mimeo-graphed sheet smelling like a school test and announcing the twentieth year reunion of my high school class. No Host Cocktail Party. Buffet Dinner. Family Picnic. Dancing. In August. Class of '58. Edison High. Stockton. My stomach is lurching. My dignity feels wobbly. I don't want to go if I'm going to be one of those without the strength to stay grown up and transcendent.

I hadn't gone to the tenth year reunion. The friends I really wanted to see, I was seeing, right? But I've been having dreams about the people in high school, and wake up with an urge to talk to them, find out how they turned out. "Did you grow up? I grew up." There are parts of myself that those people have in their keeping—they're holding things for me—different from what my new friends hold.

"When I think of you, I remember the hateful look you gave me on the day we signed yearbooks. That face has popped into my mind a few times a year for twenty years. Why did you look at me that way?" I'd like to be able to say that at the No Host Cock-tail Party. And to someone else: "I remember you winking at me across the physics lab."

I dreamed that the girl who never talked in all the years of school spoke to me: "Your house has moles living in it." Then my cat said, "I am a cat and not a car. Quit driving me around." Are there truths to be found?

Another reason I hadn't gone to my tenth was an item in the

registration form: "List your publications." Who's on the reunion
committee anyway? Somebody must have grown up to become a
personnel officer at a university. To make a list, it takes more than
an article and one poem. Cutthroat competitors. With no snooty
questions asked, maybe the classmates with interesting jail
records would show up. We are not the class to be jailed for
political activities or white collar crimes but for burglary, armed
robbery, and crimes of passion. "Reunions are planned by the
people who were popular. They want the chance to put us down
again," says a friend (Punahou Academy '68), preparing for
her tenth.

But surely, I am not going to show up this year just because
I now have a "list." And there is more to the questionnaire:
"What's the greatest happiness you've had in the last twenty
years? What do you regret the most?" I should write across the
paper, "These questions are too hard. Can I come anyway?" No,
you can't answer, "None of your business." It *is* their business;
these are the people who formed your growing up.

I have a friend (Roosevelt High '62) who refused to go to
his tenth because he had to check "married," "separated,"
"divorced," or "single." He could not bear to mark "divorced."
Family Picnic.

But another divorced friend's reunion (Roosevelt '57) turned
out to be so much fun that the class decided to meet again the
very next weekend—without the spouses, a come-without-the-
spouse party. And when my brother (Edison '60) and sister-in-

law (Edison '62) went to her reunion, there was an Old Flames Dance; you asked a Secret Love to dance. Working out the regrets, people went home with other people's spouses. Fifteen divorces and remarriages by summer's end.

At my husband Earll's (Bishop O'Dowd '56) reunion, there was an uncomfortableness as to whether to call the married priests Father or Mister or what.

What if you can't explain yourself over the loud music? Twenty years of transcendence blown away at the No Host Cocktail. Cocktails—another skill I haven't learned, like the dude in the old cowboy movies who ordered milk or lemonade or sarsaparilla. They'll have disco dancing. Never been to a disco either. Not cool after all these years.

In high school, we did not choose our friends. I sort of ended up with certain people, and then wondered why we went together. If she's the pretty one, then I must be the homely one. (When I asked my sister [Edison '59] about my "image," she said, "Well, when I think of the way you look in the halls, I picture you with your slip hanging." Not well-groomed.) We were incomplete, and made complementary friendships, like Don Quixote and Sancho Panza. Or more like the Cisco Kid and Pancho. Friendships among equals is a possibility I have found as an adult.

No, my motive for going would not be because of my "list." I was writing in high school. Writing did not protect me then, and it won't protect me now. I came from a school—no, it's not the school—it's the times; we are of a time when people don't read.

There's a race thing too. Suddenly the colored girls would walk up, and my colored girlfriend would talk and move differently. Well, they're athletes, I thought; they go to the same parties. Some years, the only place I ever considered sitting for lunch was the Chinese table. There were more of us than places at that table. Hurry and get to the cafeteria early, or go late when somebody may have finished and left a seat. Or skip lunch. We will eat with whom at the Buffet Dinner?

Earll says that he may have to work in August, and not be able to escort me. Alone at the Dance. Again.

One day, in high school, I was walking home with a popular girl. (It was poor to be seen walking to or from school by oneself.) And another popular girl, who had her own car, asked my friend to ride with her. "No, thanks," said my friend. "We'll walk." And the girl with the car stamped her foot, and said, "Come here! *We* ride home with one another." Meaning the members of their gang, I guess. The popular-girl gang. "I remember you shouting her away from me," I could say at the reunion, not, I swear, to accuse so much as to get the facts straight. Nobody had come right out and said that there were very exclusive groups of friends. They were not called "groups" or "crowds" or "gangs" or "cliques" or anything. ("Clicks," the kids today say.) "Were you in a group? Which one was I in?"

My son, who is a freshman (Roosevelt, Class of '81), says he can't make friends outside of his group. "My old friends feel left out, and then they ice me out."

What a test of character the reunion will be. I'm not worried about looks. My woman friends and I are sure that we look physically better at thirty-eight than at eighteen. By going to the reunion, I'll be able to update the looks of those people who are always eighteen in my dreams.

John Gregory Dunne (Portsmouth Priory '50) said to his wife, Joan Didion (McClatchy High '52), "It is your obligation as an American writer to go to your high school reunion." And she went. She said she dreamed about the people for a long time afterward.

I have improved: I don't wear slips anymore. I got tired of hanging around homely people. It would be nice to go to a reunion where we look at one another and know without explanations how much we improved in twenty years of life. And know that we had something to do with one another's outcomes, companions in time for a while, lucky to meet again. I wouldn't miss such a get-together for anything.

War

*T*rying to define exactly how Hawai'i is different from California, I keep coming up with the weather, though during certain seasons the weather isn't all that different. In 1967, Earll and I, with our son, left Berkeley in despair over the war. Our friends, retreating from the barricades, too, were starting communes in the northern California woods. They planned to live—to build and to plant, to marry and to have babies—as if the United States were out of Vietnam.

"Look," Lew Welch was saying, "if nobody tried to live this way, all the work of the world would be in vain." He also wrote about Chicago: "I'm just going to walk away from it. Maybe / A small part of it will die if I'm not around / feeding it anymore." That was what we felt about America.

We did not look for new jobs in Hawai'i. It was the duty of the pacifist in a war economy not to work. When you used plastic wrap or made a phone call or drank grape juice or washed your clothes or drove a car, you ran the assembly lines that delivered bombs to Vietnam.

Gary Snyder said that at the docks the forklifts make holes in sacks, and you can pick up fifteen or twenty-five pounds of rice for free once a week. We discovered that a human being could live out of the dumpsters behind the supermarkets. Blocks of cheese had only a little extra mold on them. Tear off the outer leaves, and the lettuce and cabbage heads were perfectly fresh. It wasn't until about three years ago that the supermarkets started locking their garbage bins at night.

At least the weather in Hawai'i was good for sleeping out-
doors if necessary. So it really did come down to the weather. I
remembered Defoe writing in *A Journal of the Plague Year* that
during the plague, moods were greatly affected by the weather.
Also, we had our passports ready, and if the United States com-
mitted one more unbearable atrocity, we would already be half-
way to Japan.

We discovered that O'ahu is a rim that we could drive in less
than a day. Shoes, clothes, tables, chairs washed up on the shores.
We found a ninety-dollar-a-month apartment above a grocery
store on the rim. We cadged a bunk bed from an abandoned
house, a broken park bench for a sofa, fruit and nuts but not pine-
apples because of the fifty-dollar fine. If only the war would end
before our life savings did, we would be all right. The greenery
was so lush that we did not notice for a long time that the people
were poor, that we were living in a slum by the sea.

We had not, of course, escaped from the war, but had put ourselves in the very midst of it, as close as you could get and remain
in the United States.

We should have thought of it—hardware and soldiers were
sent to Hawai'i, which funneled everything to Vietnam. Tanks
and jeeps in convoys maneuvered around the rim. Khaki soldiers
drove khaki vehicles, camouflage that did not match the bright
foliage. Like conquered natives standing on the roadside, we were
surprised when soldiers gave us the peace sign. (In Berkeley, we
hardly saw any soldiers.) We heard the target practice—with

missiles—in the mountains, where we hiked, and looked at the jagged red dirt like wounds in the earth's green skin.

At the airport, near the luggage carts, we saw coffins draped with flags. One marine per stack stood guard through the night. The coffins disappeared by day. We went to Tripler to visit a soldier we knew hurt in a motorcycle accident. He was in Neurosurgical Post Op, a ward full of young men who had been wounded in the brain. Quadriplegics. A totally paralyzed man lay on his stomach, his face toward the floor, not reading.

Soldiers came to Hawai'i for R & R. At the beach, many swimmers had various unlikely parts of their bodies bandaged. I saw three soldiers, one crippled and two bandaged, jumping in the waves with their clothes on, splashing one another, cavorting. Glad to be alive, I thought, glad to be out of Vietnam alive.

Many of the soldiers had not been wounded in Vietnam but in auto accidents here, bike accidents, swimming and surfing accidents; also they shot one another. Once out of Vietnam, they got careless, sucked through the Blowhole, drowned in the lagoons, swept away in undertows, killed the first day or week out of Vietnam. Beaten up by locals. "Swim out there," the girls said, practicing their siren ways, pointing into the Witch's Brew, the Potato Patch, the Toilet.

Paul Goodman was spending one of the last years of his life teaching in Hawai'i. Earll asked him if he were giving up working for peace. The protest was so feeble here. "No," he said, "people on all levels of power are accessible in such a small place." He wrote poems about Hawai'i: ". . . here I will never be able to make love / the people are not plain. I would be happier / trying to make out with the porpoises / if only I could swim better than I do." The newspapers cartooned him as an East Coast haole presuming to criticize paradise.

There was nothing to do but continue the protest, help the AWOL soldiers and sailors when they took sanctuary at the Church of the Crossroads and formed the Servicemen's Union. During this time, it seemed that there were more nights than days; the light came from candles and hibachis and bonfires in the Japanesy courtyard of the church. The soldiers, mere kids, illiterate boys from the poorer states, did not agree that the war was wrong; some went AWOL because they didn't like their officers, or the food was bad, or they wanted a vacation, or they were just fooling around. The peace movement was using them no less than the government was.

In the sanctuary, the peace people drilled the AWOLs in history while from outside came the voice of the Army chaplain on a bullhorn, asking them to give themselves up. Winning hearts and minds. We tried to make conversation. "What do you like to do?" I asked a short boy, who looked both stunted and hurtable in his new PX aloha shirt and the haircut that exposed his neck and ears. "I build model cars," he said. "I built five hundred of them, and I lined 'em up and shot'em and set'em on fire." "Why did you do that?" "It felt good—like when I was a door gunner on the chopper in Nam. Thousands of bullets streaming out of my gun."

Silence. Don't tell me about the gooks you shot, I thought. Don't tell me about the hootches you torched.

"What will you do next if the war doesn't end?" I asked. I did not want to keep feeding and visiting these people forever. "I don't know." Long silence. "You could go to Sweden." "Sure. That's in Canada, right? I'll help your son build model airplanes if he likes." He was comfortable playing cars with a five-year-old. He did not read the directions and glued the more intricate parts wrong. Not having the sense to stay hidden, he got into two auto accidents; we had to go to the rescue at two and three in the morning. Finally he and another boy turned themselves in at Schofield. They asked Earll to drive them. They swallowed the rest of their acid. Before they surrendered to the M.P. at the gate, they said, "Tell them you captured us. You get fifty dollars apiece reward."

The war is more or less over, but we have remained here. The military paraphernalia also remains; even our dovish members of Congress have defended Hawai'i against military cuts. But after ten years in these islands, I see through camouflages and find the winding trails inland, away from the rim. Reading Goodman's Hawai'i poems now, I hardly understand why he wanted plain loves; the world calmer, I like complexities. That his sadness seems inappropriate shows the possibility of a happier place, Hawai'i a vacation spot. I want to stay for a while to vacation.

Dishwashing

*D*ishwashing is not interesting, either to do or to think about. Thinking has dignified other mundane things, though. At least it will postpone the dishwashing, which stupefies. After eating, I look at the dishes in the sink and on the counters, the cat's dirty bowl and saucer underfoot, swipe at the dabs and smears recognizable from several meals ago, pick up a cup from among the many on chairs and beside beds, and think about suicide. Also about what to write in the suicide note.

The note is an act of kindness. The criminals who most upset us are the ones who refuse to give satisfying motives. "I don't want to wash the dishes one more time." A plain note, no hidden meanings.

I run water into the frying pan—its black underside just clears the faucet because of the pile-up—but the scrubber and the sponges are hidden somewhere in the bottom of the sink. Thwarted at the start. The frying pan fills; the pile shifts; greasy water splashes on me and spills. I turn off the water and get out of the kitchen. Let the pan soak itself clean. No way to wash the pot and the blender underneath it nor the dishes under that, the crystal wine glasses at the bottom. The dishpan and the drain are buried, too, so I can't let the cold, dirty water out. When the mood to do so overcomes me, I'll take these dishes out and start all over.

Once in a while, early in the morning, my powers at their strongest, I can enjoy washing dishes. First, reorganize the pile, then fill the dishpan again with clean water. I like water running on my wrists and the way bubbles separate from the suds and float about for quite awhile. I am the one who touches each thing, each utensil and each plate and bowl; I wipe every surface. I like putting the like items together back on the shelves. Until the next time somebody eats, I open the drawers and cupboards every few minutes to look at the neatness I've wrought.

Unfortunately, such well-being comes so rarely, and the mornings are so short, they ought not be wasted on dishes. Better to do dishes in the afternoon, "the devil's time," Tennessee Williams calls it, or in the evening immediately before dinner. The same solution for bedmaking—that is, right before going to bed. I try to limit the number of items I wash to only those needed for dinner, but since I can't find them without doing those on top, the obstructing ones get washed too. I trudge. I drudge.

The one person I know who is a worse dishwasher than I am pushes the dishes from the previous meal to the middle of the table to make places for clean saucers, no plates left.

Another person pulls a dish out of the sink and uses it as is.

When my father was a young man, working in a laundry on Mott Street in New York, he and his partners raced at meals. Last one to finish eating washed the dishes. They ate fast.

Technology is not the answer. I have had electric dishwashers, and they make little difference. The electric dishwasher does not clear the table, collect the cups from upstairs and downstairs, scrape, wipe the counters and the top of the stove. One's life has to be in an orderly phase to load and arrange the dishes inside the dishwasher. Once they're gathered in one spot like that, the momentum to do the rest of the task is fired up.

Although dishwashing is lonely work, I do not welcome assistance. With somebody else in the kitchen, I hurry to get at the worst messes to spare her or him. Alone, I wash two plates, and take a break. Helpers think that dishwashing includes unloading the dishwasher, sweeping and mopping the floor, defrosting the refrigerator, and de-crusting the oven, cleaning the kitchen, and cleaning the dining room.

In *Living Poor With Style,* Ernest Callenbach says that it is unsanitary to wipe dry because the dish cloth spreads the germs evenly over everything. Air drying is better, he says, meaning letting everything sit in the drainer. (He also recommends washing the cooking implements as you finish each step of cooking. Impossible. I did that once in a temporary state of grace, which was spoiled by having to wash dishes.)

Paper plates are no solution. There are no paper pots and pans and spatulas and mixing bowls. The plates are the easiest part of dishwashing.

I prop books and magazines behind the faucet handles. Some people have television sets in their kitchens. Books with small print are best; you don't turn the pages so often and dislodge the book into the water.

I do enjoy washing other people's dishes. I like the different dishes, different sink, different view out the window. Perhaps neighbors could move over one house each night and do one

another's dishes. You usually do other folks' dishes at a holiday
or a party.

I like using a new sponge or dishcloth or soap or gloves, but
the next time, they're not new.

In *Hawaii Over the Rainbow,* Kazuo Miyamoto says that in
the World War II relocation camps for Americans of Japanese
Ancestry, the women had the holiday of their lives—no cooking,
no dishwashing. They felt more at leisure than back home
because of the communal dining halls and camp kitchens. I can
believe it.

Compared to dishes, scrubbing the toilets is not bad, a fast job.
Also you can neglect toilets one more week, and you only have
one or two of them.

I typed a zen koan on an index card, which I have glued to the
wall beside the sink. You may cut this out and use it if you like:

> *"I have just entered the monastery. Please teach me."*
> *"Have you eaten your rice?"*
> *"I have."*
> *"Then you had better wash your bowl."*
> *At that moment, the new monk found enlightenment.*

This koan hasn't helped yet with the dishwashing; that is, no
one in the family has picked up on it. It would probably be more

enlightening to post Miyamoto or Callenbach's words. But I have a glimmering that if I solve this koan, I can solve dishwashing too. If I can solve dishwashing, I can solve life and suicide. I haven't solved it but have a few clues.

The koan does not say that the monk was enlightened after he washed the bowl. "At that moment" seems to be at the instant when he heard the advice.

I hope the koan doesn't mean that one has to pay consequences for pleasure; you eat, therefore you wash bowl. Dismal. Dismal.

It could mean something about reaching enlightenment through the quotidian, which is dishwashing.

The monk did not gain his enlightenment after washing the dishes day after day, meal after meal. Just that one bowl. Just hearing about that one bowl.

I have come up with a revolutionary meaning: Each monk in that monastery washed his own bowl. The koan suggests a system for the division of labor. Each member of the family takes his or her dishes to the sink and does them. Pots and pans negotiable. Cat dishes negotiable too.

The koan shows that dishwashing is important. A life-and-death matter, to be dealt with three times a day.

Chinaman's Hat, Oʻahu

Chinaman's Hat

*L*iving on an island, I miss driving, setting out at dawn, and ending up five or six hundred miles away—Mexico—at nightfall. Instead, we spin around and around a perimeter like on a race track.

Satellite photos of the Hawaiian Islands show swirls, currents, winds, movement, movements of clouds and water. I have to have them pointed out to me and to look closely before I descry three or four of the islands, in a clearing, chips of rock, miniatures in the very shapes you find on maps. The islands, each one the tip of a volcano connected to the ocean floor, look like the crests of waves.

Logs and glass balls have creatures living on them too. Life gathers and clings to whatever bit of solidity—land. Whales and porpoises and sharks become land for colonies of smaller animals. And the junked cars, like sunken ships, turn into living reefs.

On drives along the windward side of O'ahu, I like looking out at the ocean and seeing the pointed island offshore, not much bigger than a couple of houses—Mokoli'i Island, but nobody calls it that. I had a shock when I heard it's called Chinaman's Hat. That's what it looks like, all right, a crown and brim on the water. I had never heard "Chinaman" before except in derision when walking past racists and had had to decide whether to pretend I hadn't heard or to fight.

When driving south, clockwise around O'ahu, there is an interesting optical illusion: at a certain point in the road, the sky is

covered with Chinaman's Hat, which looms huge, near. The
closer you drive toward what seems like a mountain ahead, the
farther it moves away until there it is, quite far off, a small island
in the midst of ocean, sky, clouds.

I did not call it Chinaman's Hat, and no one else calls it
Mokoli'i Island, so for a long time, I didn't call it anything.
"Chinaman's Hat," people say to visitors, "because it looks just
like a Chinaman's hat. See?"

And the visitor knows right away what they mean. At first I
watched expressions and tones of voice for a snide reference to
me. But the locals were not yelling at me or spitting at me or
trying to run me down with a bike saying, "Chinaman."

Although I don't swim very well, I ventured out to Chinaman's Hat three times. The first time, we waited until low tide to
walk as far as we could. The other times, we left in the early
morning. Snorkeling is like flying; the moment your face enters
clear water, you become a flying creature.

Schools of fish—zebra fish, rainbow fish, red fish—curve
with the currents, swim alongside and away. Balloon fish puff out
their porcupine quills. How unlike a dead fish a live fish is. We
swam through spangles of silver white fish. I hovered in perfect
suspension over forests, flew over spring forests and winter
forests. No sound but my own breathing. Sometimes we entered
blind spots, darkness, where the sand churned up gray fog, the
sun behind clouds. Then I had to lift my head out of the water to
see and not be afraid.

Sometimes the sun made golden rooms, which we entered
from dark hallways. Specks of sand shone like gold and fell like
motes, like the light in California. Sea cucumbers rocked from
side to side.

Approaching Chinaman's Hat, there is a group of tall black
stones like an underwater Stonehenge, and we flew around and
between those rocks.

Then we were walking among the palm trees and bushes that
we had seen from O'ahu. Under those bushes, large white birds
nest on the ground. We hurried to the unseen side of the island,
the other face of the moon.

Though tiny, Chinaman's Hat has its leeward and windward.
The ocean side is less green but wonderful in its variety. We
found a cave, a tiny pirate's cove with a lick of ocean going in and
out of it; a strip of beach made of fine yellow sand; a blowhole;
brown and lavender cowry shells, not broken; black live crabs and
red dead crabs; a lava rock shelf with tide pools as warm as baths.
Lying in a tide pool, I saw nothing but sky and black rock; the
ocean spit cold now and again. The two friends with us stood in
the blowhole, and said wedding vows while the ocean sprayed
rainbows around their heads.

At day's end, tired from the long swim at high tide, we pulled
ourselves up on the land, lay with arms open holding on to O'ahu.
We were grateful to return, relieved that we had made it back
alive. Relieved to be out of the water before the sun went down.

After that first exploration, we heard from Hawaiians that the channel between Chinaman's Hat and Oʻahu is the spawning place for sharks. This information did not stop us from swimming out there twice more. We had the fatalism of city people who had lived on the San Andreas Fault. It will crack open at any moment, and California break off from North America, and sink like Atlantis. We continued to swim home with the fish we'd caught tied to our belts, and they did not attract sharks though pilot fish swam ahead of us.

The air of Hawaiʻi breathes warm on the skin; when it blows, I seem to turn into wind, too, and start to blow away. Maybe I can swim because the water is so comfortable, I melt into it and let it carry me like the fish and the frigate birds that make the currents visible. Back on Oʻahu, our friend who got married in the blow-hole, often broke into hysterics, and she and her husband returned to the cool northern California woods.

There is a rending. The soul leaks out to mix with the air, the skin an osmotic membrane. But the eyes squint against the bright green foliage in the red light. These islands fool human beings into thinking that they are safe. On our second trip to Chinaman's Hat, a Hawaiian man and his son were camping under the ledge by the palm trees. They had a boat and meat hooks and liver for catching sharks.

On the third trip, Earll went spear fishing off the ocean side, where I did not go because of the depth and choppiness. I was climbing as far as I could up the crown, and finding seashells there. I watched him jump vertically out of the water. He had seen a giant thing and felt it swim under him, yards and yards of brown shadow under him.

Another time, we rowed a boat out there, our children sitting on the outrigger to weight it down on the water. A cleft in the hillside made a shelter for building a fire to get warm after swimming. At sunset, we cooked and ate the fish the men speared. We were climbing down to the boat, holding on to the face of the island in the dark, when a howling like wolves, like ghosts, came rising out of the island. "Birds," somebody said. "The wind," said someone else. But the air was still, and the high, clear sound wound like a ribbon around the island. It was, I know it, the island, the voice of the island singing, the sirens Odysseus heard.

The Navy uses Kaho'olawe for bombing practice, not recognizing it as living, sacred earth. We had all heard it, the voice of our island singing.

A City Person Encountering Nature

A city person encountering nature hardly recognizes it, has no patience for its cycles, and disregards animals and plants unless they roar and exfoliate in spectacular aberrations. Preferring the city myself, I can better discern natural phenomena when books point them out; I also need to verify what I think I've seen, even though charts of phyla and species are orderly whereas nature is wild, unruly.

Last summer, my friend and I spent three days together at a beach cottage. She got up early every morning to see what "critters" the ocean washed up. The only remarkable things I'd seen at that beach in years were Portuguese man-o-war and a flightless bird, big like a pelican; the closer I waded toward it, the farther out to sea the bird bobbed.

We found flecks of whitish gelatin, each about a quarter of an inch in diameter. The wet sand was otherwise clean and flat. The crabs had not yet dug their holes. We picked up the blobs on our fingertips and put them in a saucer of sea water along with seaweeds and some branches of coral.

One of the things quivered, then it bulged, unfolded, and flipped over or inside out. It stretched and turned over like a human being getting out of bed. It opened and opened to twice its original size. Two arms and two legs flexed, and feathery wings flared, webbing the arms and legs to the body, which tapered to a graceful tail. Its ankles had tiny wings on them—like Mercury. Its back muscles were articulated like a comic book superhero's—blue and silver metallic leotards outlined with black racing stripes. It's a spaceman, I thought. A tiny spaceman in a spacesuit.

I felt my mind go wild. A little spaceship had dropped a spaceman on to our planet. The other blob went through its gyrations and also metamorphosed into a spaceman. I felt as if I were having the flying dream where I watch two perfect beings wheel in the sky.

The two critters glided about, touched the saucer's edges. Suddenly, the first one contorted itself, turned over, made a bulge like an octopus head, then flipped back, streamlined again. A hole in its side—a porthole, a vent—opened and shut. The motions happened so fast, we were not certain we had seen them until both creatures had repeated them many times.

I had seen similar quickenings: dry strawberry vines and dead trout revive in water. Leaves and fins unfurl; colors return.

We went outside to catch more, and, our eyes accustomed, found a baby critter. So there were more than a pair of these in the universe. So they grew. The baby had apparently been in the sun too long, though, and did not revive.

The next morning, bored that the critters were not performing more tricks, we blew on them to get them moving. By accident, their eyes or mouths faced, and sucked together. There was a churning. They wrapped their arms, legs, wings around one another.

Not knowing whether they were killing each other or mating, we tried unsuccessfully to part them. Guts, like two worms, came out of the portholes. Intestines, I thought; they're going to die. But the two excrescences braided together like DNA strands, then whipped apart, turned pale, and smokily receded into the holes. The critters parted, flipped, and floated away from each other.

After a long time, both of them fitted their armpits between the coral branches; we assumed that they were depositing eggs.

When we checked the clock, four hours had gone by. We'd both thought it had only been about twenty minutes.

That afternoon, the creatures seemed less distinct, their sharp lines blurring. I rubbed my eyes; the feathers were indeed melting. The beings were disintegrating in the water. I threw the coral as far out as I could into the ocean.

Later, back in town, we showed our biologist friend our sketches, I burbling about visitors from outer space. He said they were nudibranchs. This was our friend who as a kid had vowed that he would study Nature, but in college, he specialized in marine biology, and in graduate school, he studied shrimps. He was now doing research on one species of shrimp that he had discovered on one reef off O'ahu.

A new climate helps me to see nature. Here are some sights upon moving to Hawai'i:

Seven black ants, led by an orange one, dismembered a fly.

I peeled sunburn off my nose, and later recognized it as the flake of something an ant was marching away with.

A mushroom grew in a damp corner of the living room.

Giant philodendrons tear apart the cars abandoned in the

jungle. Tendrils crawl out of the hoods; they climb the shafts of
the steam shovels that had dug the highway. Roofs and trunks
break open, turn red, orange, brown, and sag into the dirt.

Needing to read explanations of such strangeness, we bought
an English magazine, *The Countryman,* which reports "The Wild
Life and Tame" news.

"STAMPED TO DEATH — A hitherto peaceful herd of about fifty
cows, being fetched in from pasture, suddenly began to rush
around, and bellow in a most alarming manner. The source of
their interest was a crippled gull, which did its best to escape;
but the cows, snorting and bellowing, trampled it to death. They
then quieted down and left the field normally.—Charles Brudett,
Hants."

Also: "BIG EYE, Spring, 1967—When I was living in the
Karoo, a man brought me a five-foot cape cobra which he had
just killed. It had been unusually sluggish and the tail of another
snake protruded from its mouth. This proved to be a boom-
slang, also poisonous but back-fanged; it was 1½ inches longer
than the cobra and its head-end had been partly digested.
—J. S. Taylor, Fife."

I took some students to the zoo after reading Blake's "Tyger,
Tyger burning bright," Stevens's "Thirteen Ways of Looking at a
Blackbird," and Lorenz's *King Solomon's Ring.* They saw the
monkeys catch a pigeon and tear it apart. I kept reminding them
that that was extraordinary. "Watch an animal going about its
regular habits," I said, but then they saw an alligator shut its jaws

on a low-flying pigeon. I remembered that I don't see ordinary stuff either.

I've watched ants make off with a used Band-Aid. I've watched a single termite bore through a book, a circle clean through. I saw a pigeon vomit milk, and didn't know whether it was sick, or whether its babies had died and the milk sacs in its throat were engorged. I have a friend who was pregnant at the same time as her mare, and, just exactly like the Chinese superstition that only one of the babies would live, the horse gave birth to a foal in two pieces.

When he was about four, we took our son crabbing for the "crabs with no eyes," as he called them. They did have eyes, but they were on stalks. The crabs fingered the bait as if with hands; very delicately they touched it, turned it, swung it. One grabbed hold of the line, and we pulled it up. But our son, a Cancer, said, "Let's name him Linda." We put Linda back in the river and went home.

Useful Education

I have taught school for twelve years. I've taught grammar school, high school, alternative school, business school, and college; math, English, English as a second language, journalism, and creative writing. I've also been a writer for twenty-eight years, the writing years and the teaching years over-lapping. I ought to be able to tell how to teach people to write.

The way I don't do it is the way Mrs. Garner taught us in fourth grade. Mrs. Garner was an organized woman, who brought out a box of decorations for each holiday and new season. Year after year, she put up the same bulletin boards and gave the same lessons; we knew exactly what the younger brother or sister was learning and what would come next. Nowadays we teachers invent new courses each semester—The American Novel in Film, Science Fiction, The Alienated Adolescent, Lovers at War, etc. We never get to establish a file of tried and true ditto sheets like Mrs. Garner's. She pressed hers on a gelatin plate, and pulled duplicates one by one.

It was her tradition to have us make a notebook entitled *Gems*. She did not explain what "gems" were. The only other time we used that word was in "Columbia, the Gem of the Ocean," one of her favorite songs. The notebook was not about jewels, nor is "Columbia, the Gem of the Ocean." She let us pick out our own construction paper for the cover; I chose a pink nubby oatmeal paper, and lettered "Gems" in lime green. While we were numbering the pages the way she showed us, she stuck chalk into the fingers of the wood-and-wire rakelike thing that enabled

her to draw five straight lines at one stroke. She usually made
musical scales with it, but for "gems," she ran it back and forth
until the blackboard looked like a sheet of binder paper. Then
she wrote a "gem," which we were to copy word for word and
line for line, indenting and breaking the lines the way she did.
Perhaps the "gems" were a penmanship lesson, I thought, but
wasn't that when we drew loops and zigzags? Copying the
"gems" was like art period, when she drew an apple on the board
with red chalk, then a brown stem with a green leaf shooting off
to the right. We copied this apple as exactly as we could, and she
corrected our shapes with her art pencil. She had a drawer filled
with the comic books she confiscated, another drawer of water
pistols and another of slingshots. If I were to use her methods
today, the students would beat me up. (I once confiscated some
nunchakus, a pair of night sticks on a chain, which I put in my
desk drawer.)

And yet it was in Mrs. Garner's classroom that I discovered
that I could write poems. I remember the very moment the room
filled with a light that would have been white except that the
warm light off the wooden desks (with the inkwell holes and the
pencil grooves) suffused it with yellow—and out of the air and
into my head and down my arm and out my fingers came ten,
twenty verses in an a-b-b-a rhyme. The poem was about flying;
I flew.

I was supposed to have been writing the multiplication tables
or making our daily copy of the map of California. We had to

draw every squiggle in the coastline. How lucky the fourth graders in Colorado are, we said. Instead I wrote down the music and the voices I heard. So, as a teacher, when I see students staring at nothing, I am loathe to interrupt.

One of my students who is now a published poet, Jody Manabe, said that she quit writing for one year because her seventh-grade teacher, a man, told her, "You write like a man."

The best I ever wrote in high school was when the teachers said, "Write whatever you like." Now I can appreciate what a daring assignment that is. I would not like to be caught saying that when an administrator or department head walks in to see if I have lesson plans.

The worst writing happened during the four years of college, which I attended when the English departments were doing the New Criticism (and the art department, Abstract Expressionism). The rule at our school was that an undergraduate could take one creative writing class, and she had to wait until junior or senior year. Poems, short stories, plays, and novels were what great masters wrote and what we students wrote about. We wrote essays.

The school system is dominated by the essay. And for me, essays would not become poems or stories. The real writing got stalled until after homework and graduation. The only place I could be fanciful was in the title. The professors wrote, "Purple prose," next to the few interesting phrases I could squeeze into "the body." Looking back on it, I believe the essay form was what drove English majors into becoming the most vituperative demonstrators during the student strikes.

My favorite method for teaching writing is to have the students write any old way. I tell them I "grade by quantity and not quality." By writing a hundred pages per semester, they have to improve—and the writing will find its form.

I tell the students that form—the epic, the novel, drama, the various forms of poetry—is organic to the human body. Petrarch did not invent the sonnet. Human heartbeat and language and voice and breath produce these rhythms. The teacher can look at a student's jumble of words and say, "I see you are moving toward the short story," or whatever. This is a good way to criticize and compliment—tell the young writer how close he or she is getting to which form.

To begin with form would probably work, too, as long as it's not the essay. Put a problem into a sonnet and it will help you state the problem, explore it, and solve it elegantly in a couplet. Ballads come naturally to students, who are lyric, and young like Keats and Shelley.

In *The Catcher in the Rye,* Holden takes an Oral Expression class where the students have to give spontaneous speeches, and whenever a speaker digresses, the class and Mr. Vinson yell, "Digression!" Sometimes the speaker can hardly talk anymore and gets an F. Mr. Vinson doesn't know that if you let somebody digress long enough, what he says will eventually take shape, a classical shape.

As a teacher, I have a stake in controlling that classroom, too. And the essay is orderly, easy to write and easy to grade; a computer can do it. Just check the thesis statement and make sure that each major paragraph backs up the thesis with arguments, examples, and quotes.

I do teach the essay—the three-paragraph essay, then the five-paragraph essay, then the term paper—so that my students can survive college. I try to throw in enough other kinds of writing to put the essay in perspective. When the class is over, though, kids probably forget everything but the essay. It is a form that the brain grasps. But if I become paralyzed worrying about the kid writers I am damaging, I try to remember how tough writers are. Kwan Kung, the god of war and literature, rides before us.

Talk Story: A Writers' Conference

*T*wo weeks ago, I went to Talk Story, the first conference of Asian American and Hawai'i writers. Never before had I listened to writers read and talk for a week straight, taking time out for eating and sleeping, but usually talking about writing while eating, too. It takes me about twenty years to see meaning in events, but here are some first impressions:

The opening party was at Washington Place, the Governor's mansion, where Queen Lili'uokalani stayed under house arrest in 1895. We ladies trailed our long skirts over the lawns and through the rooms of Victorian furniture to the lanai, where the band and the food and wine were. People blessed one another with leis and kisses, and the smell and the music of Hawai'i filled the air. The moon, full that very night, rolled out of the rushing clouds. I didn't get to the food because I was dazzled by meeting the people whom I had only imagined from their writings.

The writers from the mainland, not used to Hawai'i, must have felt strange, having just come out of their solitary writing rooms.

Listening to the keynote speakers the next morning, I was humbled when Ozzie Bushnell, author of *Ka'a'awa*, said that if "us local kids" don't write the Hawai'i novel, then "the outsider" will come in and do it. I guiltily identified with this "outsider." Ozzie is such a strong speaker, talking both standard English and pidgin, that I felt scolded, a Captain Cook of literature, plundering the islands for metaphors, looting images, distorting the landscape with a mainland—a mainstream—viewpoint. I temporarily forgot my trusty superstition: the capable seer needs only a glimpse of the room or the forest or the city to describe it and its inhabitants more truly than one who has lived there always. A place gives no special writing powers to those born and raised in it.

On the second day, during the panel, "The Plantations and the World War II Camp Experience," Noriko Bridges read the one poem she has taken a lifetime to write. She wept in the middle of it, where the brothers are killed fighting in Europe, their families still imprisoned; many listeners cried too, some women holding hands. Writers who had not seen one another since camp days were having a reunion. They had first published in the camp newsletters.

There was a lovely moment when Milton Murayama, author of *All I Asking for Is My Body,* talked about how pidgin vocabulary is changing. For example, nowadays, Hawai'i people say, "good," "mo' bettah," and "da best." But in the old days, they said, "good," "go-o-od," and "go-o-o-o-od!" He said the "goods" louder and louder and louder.

On the third day, we Chinese Americans had a fight. Two of the panelists were Jeff Paul Chan and Shawn Wong, editors of the anthology, *Aiiieeeee!,* who said that publishers maintain a ghetto of female ethnic autobiographers and reject the work of male ethnic novelists. They said that the known bulk of Chinese American literature consists of nine autobiographies, seven by women. We are to draw the conclusion that the dominant society uses minority women to castrate the men. The audience was very upset. Some felt insulted at the speakers' proud use of the word "Chinaman." Lilah Kan from New York came bursting forth with her beautiful gray hair flying, to accuse the panelists of being part of a "Chinese American literary mafia."

Afterward, my feminist friends said we should have cheered for those seven women. The newspapers said the "brawl" was between the mainland Chinese Americans and the island Chinese Americans. But I think it was the men against the women—the men erecting Louis Chu, male novelist, as the father figure by knocking down the Jade Snow Wong mother figure. It was embarrassing that we were the only ethnic group that did not show a harmonious face; on the other hand, I felt good about our liveliness.

On the fourth afternoon, I moderated the panel, "Themes and Concerns of Writers in Hawai'i." Probably because of the events of the previous day, people kept interpreting this title politically, but none of the panelists wanted to or could talk that way. Phyllis Hoge Thompson, speaking from the audience, said she had set out to write a poem about Tom Gill losing the election for Governor. "But the poem turned out to be about a tree in the snow," she said. "Holding" is about the Scandinavian Yggdrasil tree, though even the name of the tree doesn't appear. She was mapping the strange, secret way of poetry, and I wished she were on the panel instead of me, an "outsider."

The most wondrous presentations were two evenings given by

the Hawaiians, who each gave his or her genealogy of teachers. They chanted and danced variations of the same mele, sometimes accompanied by gourd and sometimes by knee drums, for example. They told how a new mele is written today, often first in English, then translated into Hawaiian by a teacher, who tells the poet what kind of a mele it is (an Entrance poem, a Call, etc.), and where it belongs in tradition.

The panelists' families and students sat in the back of the auditorium, and after the program, the children walked up to the stage and sang for their teacher, John Kaha'i Topolinski. Some participants who had attended the two previous Asian American Writers' Conferences (Oakland '75 and Seattle '76) said that the Hawaiians were contributing the only new theory and scholarship. The Hawaiians also gave a vision of the artist, not as anchorite but as builder of community.

Voice after voice telling all manner of things, by Saturday, I found myself saying my own work inside my head to counteract certain poets. My ears and head and body rejected their beats, which I also tried to cancel by tapping out my own rhythms with a finger. I felt like Johnny-Got-His-Gun, paralyzed except for that one finger. Earll, my husband, was reciting Yeats's poetry to himself, as antidote.

A rhythm that is wrong for you might stop your heart, or, anyway, scramble your brain. I learned that it is not story or idea that counts. What really matters is the music. A famous writer walked out as I read my suspenseful new chapter. (" 'Nothing but disdain,' Mimi thought, 'could make some Chinese passionate.' "—Diana Chang in *The Frontiers of Love*.) I watched her high-heeled silhouette dart out of the lighted doorway. She probably prevented my rhythms from breaking up hers. Or maybe she needed sleep; it was almost midnight.

At the last set of readings Saturday night, Ninotchka Rosca was nowhere to be found. The rumor spread among the writers that she was at work on her novel; the writing was coming to her that night, and she would not interrupt it. We enviously told one another this story of discipline, dedication, and nerve. We could have been making the story up in a fit of withdrawal symptoms, having abandoned our writing for a week.

Hundreds of us went to the lūʻau at the Sumida Watercress Farm Sunday evening. I felt a shock to see Stephen Sumida exhume the pig—pink and long like a human being   the dirt and burlap falling away. Will there now be a cycle of pig imagery in our work? How do reality and writing connect anyway?

I know at least six people who fell in love at first sight during the conference—all requited—levels and levels of conferring.

A according to mystical people, spiritual forces converge at Hawai'i, as do ocean currents and winds. Kāhuna, keepers and teachers of the old religion and arts (such as song writing, the hula, navigation, taro growing), still work here. The islands attract refugee lamas from Tibet, and the Dalai Lama and the Black Hat Lama have visited them. Some kāhuna say they see tree spirits fly from branch to branch; the various winds and rains are spirits, too; sharks and rocks have spirits. If ancestors and immortals travel on supernatural errands between China and the Americas, they must rest here in transit, nothing but ocean for thousands of miles around. They landed more often in the old days, before the sandalwood trees were cut down.

Whether it was because I listened to too many ghost stories or was born sensitive to presences, I spent about three years of childhood in helpless fear of the supernatural. I saw a whirling witch in the intersection by our house. She had one red cheek and one black cheek. Surrounded by a screaming, pointing crowd, she turned and turned on her broom. Maybe she was only somebody in a Hallowe'en costume when I didn't know about Hallowe'en, but she put me into torment for years. I was afraid of cat eyes at night. Wide-eyed with insomnia, I listened in the dark to voices whispering, chains dragging and clanging, footsteps coming my way.

At about the same kidtime, Earll saw a little witch dancing on his dresser. Hoping to help our son become a fearless down-to-

earth person, we have raised Joseph secularly. We explain things
to him logically.

Joseph had already gotten through his babyhood when we
came to Hawaiʻi; he would seem no longer in danger of succumb-
ing to the fear of ghosts. But Hawaiʻi, new land which has
recently risen out of the water, has overwhelming animism; that
is, it seems more alive than cities which have been paved over for
hundreds of years. Or Joseph developed his sixth sense at a later
age than we did, and, person and place coming together, he
started to see things.

Even our friends with Ph.D.s see things in Hawaiʻi. Our friend
from Minnesota kept telling us about the row of fishermen walking in the ocean with torches at night. "They're chanting to attract
the fish," he said. Later, he learned he was describing the march
of the dead warriors. Another sensible friend tells us how he ran
from block to block to dodge the nightwalkers. "I would've died
if they crossed my path," he said. The most unimaginative people
hear the hoofbeats of the princess's horse, and lock their doors.
They wrestle with invisible foes at ceremonial grounds, see—and
photograph—the face of the goddess Pele in the volcano fire,
offer the old woman—Pele in disguise—water when she comes
asking for it, floating on smoking feet.

We were driving one day when I caught a sign that Joseph
was not the simple little boy I had hoped for. He held his head,
shaking it, and crying out, "I can't stand it. The thoughts are
moving so fast in there." I didn't like that; he felt his thoughts

apart from himself; the very process of thinking hurt him. With my hands on the wheel, I gave inadequate comfort.

One night I heard him walking about, and in the morning he said he had seen a light come over the top of the wall. (The wall of his room didn't join the ceiling.) He had gotten up to shut off the light. What he saw in the living room was one window lit up and a man standing in it. The glow was coming from the man. We lived on the second floor.

When he was about twelve, and should have been old enough to have outgrown his fancifulness, he came home early in the morning and jumped shaking into bed. He and his friends had been playing at a construction site before the workers came. Hiding from one another, he had lost his friends and was running home when he saw a Menehune, one of the little people of Hawai'i, standing on a lava rock fence. "It had a shiny crown on its head," he said, "and its mouth opened and opened until there was nothing but this big hollow in its face. Its head moved like this, following me." He tells about this laughing Menehune as factually as he tells a math problem, without self-dramatization or doubt.

Months afterward, he wasn't sleeping well; he kept groaning and tossing. "You know the voices calling your name before you go to sleep?" he said. "I usually like listening to them. But lately they've been very loud, and I don't like their sound." I was alarmed that he thought that everyone has voices, though pleasant ones, calling them. "The voices are coming out of the closet."

And I noticed that the closet door kept opening. I would shut it myself when he went to bed, and when I checked on him, I'd find it open.

Without mentioning it, he bought five pounds of rock salt with his own money and sprinkled it all over the house; Hawaiians do that to stop hauntings.

I remembered Chinese stories about voices calling, and the lesson would be that you mustn't answer when you hear your name. You mustn't follow the voices. I recalled Goethe's poem about the Erl-king's daughter. To find guidance, you have to use the lore that science scoffs at. If Joseph had started being afraid of bats, we would have hung garlic around his neck and around the house.

I pulled his ears while calling his name and address the way my mother did for us after nightmares. He helped me seal the closet door with good Chinese words on red paper. We found a cross that had been part of a theatrical costume, also an ankh and scarab, replicas from the Metropolitan Museum of Art, and hung them from the doorknob. We picked ti leaves and strewed his room with them.

Joseph had a few quiet nights, and we thought the strangeness was over. But then I found him standing in the hallway shivering in the hot afternoon. He said that something had come out of the closet and was in the hallway. "The cold spot is here," he said. "I'm standing in the middle of it. I'm fighting it." That spot did not feel odd to me.

We asked our friend from Thailand what to do, and she gave us a medallion of a saint for him to wear around his neck, and also a little stone Buddha that Thais wear in a gold box. She said he should put the Buddha by his head when he went to bed. It had been handed down in her family, which have been rulers and rebels of Thailand. Joseph has had no more supernatural disturbances.

In a way it's a shame to have him put his powers away, fold his wings, but those abilities are not needed in America in the twentieth century.

The writers' conference I went to ended with a kahuna who helped us perform ho'oponopono; all animosities would be resolved. Fewer people stayed for that event than any other. Maybe in ancient Hawai'i, a kahuna like this one would have trained Joseph, whose tendencies would have become useful. She asked us to shut our eyes and hold hands in a circle; she talked to us calmly, saying that a column of light was entering the circle. I opened my eyes to peek, to check out the reality of that column. There was indeed a column of light, but also a skylight in the roof that let it in. The way the world works now, Joseph needs to learn to see the skylight, too.

Fire in the sea.
The Big Island, Hawai'i.

Lew Welch: An Appreciation

N ot everybody who writes poems knows what a poem is. Lew Welch knew. I'm glad I got to meet him before he disappeared. He's often called a San Francisco poet or a California poet. He studied music in Stockton. He lived with his wife, Magda, in a house on a slope in Marin City, which is a Black city.

They had been expecting Earll and me; Magda had made enough sandwiches for about ten people, then went outside to work in her garden. She probably fed lots of kid poets who came to see her husband. Being still young, we naturally expected food and attention from adults, and did not recognize largesse when we received it. Lew Welch then was working at the docks as a longshoremen's clerk, and now that I'm a worker and a writer myself, I know better than to take up a man's time on his day off.

He had cut his red hair for the summer. He had written about that: "In summer I usually cut it all off. / I do it myself, with scissors and a / little Jim Beam." He looked exactly as he said in his poem:

> *Not yet 40, my beard is already white.*
> *Not yet awake, my eyes are puffy and red,*
> *like a child who has cried too much.*

Only, I think, he had reached forty already; he had lines in his face, but though his eyes were red, they opened wide. He looked at you out of bright blue eyes, but at a part of you that isn't your appearance or even your personality; he addressed that part of you that is like everybody. I would like to learn to look at people that way.

He went for his papers and books and got down to business. He read to us. He cried. He sang:

> *She bared her bos'm*
> *I whupped out m'knife*
> *Carved my initials on her thin breast bone.*

"I invented putting a note before and after the parts that need to be sung," he said. "The book has these fussy sixteenth notes because those were the only notes the printer had. They should have been quarter notes." I admired his caring about detail, and have checked the editions of his work that were printed after he disappeared, to see if the notes had been changed. They had, and they do look better.

He read a poem about driving, written by one of his students, and said, "Now, there's a poem. There's a poet. I phoned him to come do a reading with me, but he had to work on his car." There was going to be a reading that weekend by the Bay Area's best-known poets. "That's cool. That's right. He ought to be working on his car."

From the window, you could see down the hill to a round space filled with motorcycles and cars with their hoods up. Kids were repairing them. "Somebody ought to subsidize garages all over the country, stocked with automotive tools," he said. "Kids can come work on their cars, something real, when they drop out of school."

He had many ideas for things for you to do. There is a poem accompanied by a circle drawn in one brushstroke. The poem is in his clear handwriting. He read it as if it were a friendly but imperative suggestion:

> *Step out onto the planet*
> *Draw a circle a hundred feet round.*
> *Inside the circle are*
> *300 things nobody understands, and, maybe,*
> *nobody's ever really seen.*
> *How many can you find?*

One of his ideas was to organize to feed poets "so poets could have babies and fix their wives' teeth and the other things we need." He planned a magazine to be called *Bread* that would discuss the economics of being a poet in America. Somebody still needs to carry out these plans.

He talked about being one of the young poets who had driven William Carlos Williams from the airport to Reed College. I love the way that car ride has become a part of literary history. Gary Snyder, Lew Welch, Philip Whalen, and William Carlos Williams were the poets in the car. Today, Welch told us that he had felt

Williams giving the power of poetry to him. The two of them had agreed on their dislike of T. S. Eliot.

Then Lew Welch sang us "The Waste Land" to a jive beat, and it did not sound at all as if he disliked it.

He said that poetry has to be useful. He was very proud that the No Name Bar in Sausalito pasted in its window his poem for protecting the town, and the "innkeeper" published that poem, "Sausalito Trash Prayer" by duplicating forty copies of it and giving it to people. It was "pasted in the florist's window . . . carefully retyped and put right out there on Divisadero Street . . . that it might remind of love, that it might sell flowers. . . ."

He read "After Anacreon," a poem about cab driving. He said that he had also read it to his fellow Yellow Cab drivers, and was happy when they told him that that was exactly what being a cabby is like.

He didn't say it that day, but there's some practical advice of his that is told by one to another, a word-of-mouth poem: "Think Jewish, dress Black, drive Okie."

He was a wise and trustworthy man. He warned and comforted kid writers: "To become enamored of our powers is to lose them, at once!" ". . . full / full of my gift / I am only / left out and afraid." He wrote two poems he called the first American koans, "The Riddle of Hands" and "The Riddle of Bowing." He invited readers who solved these koans to have their answers confirmed by writing to him. There was flesh behind his words.

I guess that's why he was willing to see us, and also why he looked so worn.

After about two hours, we had to go, a sense of urgency about the work to be done having come over us. We thanked him and Magda for the poems and the beer and sandwiches, and said goodbye.

I haven't told you much that you can't read for yourself. He had spoken exactly like his writing.

I encourage my own students to write in dialect, and give them Lew Welch's instructions on how to do it: "Dialect is only a regional and personal voiceprint. . . . You can easily separate structure and meaning from dialect, and still be dealing with sound, with music, with speech, with another's Mind. Gertrude Stein perfectly mimicked the rhythms and structures of Baltimore Blacks in her story 'Melanctha' and she didn't transcribe the dialect at all—that is, didn't have to misspell a lot of words to get the work done. Nelson Algren has many many passages with no misspellings, but he catches the real flow of regional speech."

I keep some Lew Welch advice over my desk: "When I write, my only concern is accuracy. I try to write accurately from the poise of mind which lets us see that things are exactly what they seem. I never worry about beauty, if it is accurate there is always beauty. I never worry about form, if it is accurate there is always form." I ditto this for my students at the beginnings of courses, and tell them I have not much more to teach them, but they don't believe me, and stay.

In the spring of 1971, Lew Welch walked away into the woods of Nevada County, and has not come back. His editor, Donald Allen, compiled and published *Ring of Bone: Collected Poems 1950–1971.* Allen ended his editor's note: "O.K., Lew, I've done what you asked me to do. And, now, where are you?"

A Sea Worry

*T*his summer our son bodysurfs. He says it's his "job" and rises each morning at 5:30 to catch the bus to Sandy Beach. I hope that by September he will have had enough of the ocean. Tall waves throw surfers against the shallow bottom. Undertows have snatched them away. Sharks prowl Sandy's. Joseph told me that once he got out of the water because he saw an enormous shark. "Did you tell the life guard?" I asked. "No." "Why not?" "I didn't want to spoil the surfing." The ocean pulls at the boys, who turn into surfing addicts. At sunset you can see surfers waiting for the last golden wave.

"Why do you go surfing so often?" I ask my students.

"It feels so good," they say. "Inside the tube. I can't describe it. There are no words for it."

"You can describe it," I scold, and I am angry. "Everything can be described. Find the words for it, you lazy boy. Why don't you stay home and read?" I am afraid that the boys give themselves up to the ocean's mindlessness.

When the waves are up, surfers all over Hawai'i don't do their homework. They cut school. They know how the surf is breaking at any moment because every fifteen minutes the reports come over the radio; in fact, one of my former students is the surf reporter.

Some boys leave for mainland colleges, and write their parents heartrending letters. They beg to come home for Thanksgiving. "If I can just touch the ocean," they write from Missouri and Kansas, "I'll last for the rest of the semester." Some come home for Christmas and don't go back.

Even when the assignment is about something else, the students write about surfing. They try to describe what it is to be inside the wave as it curls over them, making a tube or "chamber" or "green room" or "pipeline" or "time warp." They write about the silence, the peace, "no hassles," the feeling of being reborn as they shoot out the end. They've written about the voice of God, the "commandments" they hear. In the margins, they draw the perfect wave. Their writing is full of clichés. "The endless summer," they say. "Unreal."

Surfing is like a religion. Among the martyrs are George Helm, Kimo Mitchell, and Eddie Aikau. Helm and Mitchell were lost at sea riding their surfboards from Kahoʻolawe, where they had gone to protest the Navy's bombing of that island. Eddie Aikau was a champion surfer and lifeguard. A storm had capsized the Hōkūleʻa, the ship that traces the route that the Polynesian ancestors sailed from Tahiti, and Eddie Aikau had set out on his board to get help.

Since the ocean captivates our son, we decided to go with him to see Sandy's.

We got up before dawn, picked up his friend, Marty, and drove out of Honolulu. Almost all the traffic was going in the opposite direction, the freeway coned to make more lanes into the city. We came to a place where raw mountains rose on our left and the sea fell on our right, smashing against the cliffs. The strip of cliff pulverized into sand is Sandy's. "Dangerous Current Exist," said the ungrammatical sign.

Earll and I sat on the shore with our blankets and thermos of coffee. Joseph and Marty put on their fins and stood at the edge of the sea for a moment, touching the water with their fingers and crossing their hearts before going in. There were fifteen boys out there, all about the same age, fourteen to twenty, all with the same kind of lean, v-shaped build, most of them with black hair that made their wet heads look like sea lions. It was hard to tell whether our kid was one of those who popped up after a big wave. A few had surfboards, which are against the rules at a bodysurfing beach, but the lifeguard wasn't on duty that early.

As they watched for the next wave, the boys turned toward the ocean. They gazed slightly upward; I thought of altar boys before a great god. When a good wave arrived, they turned, faced shore, and came shooting in, some taking the wave to the right and some to the left, their bodies fishlike, one arm out in front, the hand and fingers pointed before them, like a swordfish's beak. A few held credit card trays, and some slid in on trays from MacDonald's.

"That is no country for middle-aged women," I said. We had on bathing suits underneath our clothes in case we felt moved to participate. There were no older men either.

Even from the shore, we could see inside the tubes. Sometimes, when they came at an angle, we saw into them a long way. When the wave dug into the sand, it formed a brown tube or a gold one. The magic ones, though, were made out of just water, green and turquoise rooms, translucent walls and ceilings. I saw one that was powder-blue, perfect, thin; the sun filled it with sky blue and white light. The best thing, the kids say, is when you are in the middle of the tube, and there is water all around you but you're dry.

The waves came in sets; the boys passed up the smaller ones. Inside a big one, you could see their bodies hanging upright, knees bent, duckfeet fins paddling, bodies dangling there in the wave.

Once in a while, we heard a boy yell, "Aa-whoo!" "Poon-tah!" "Aaroo!" And then we noticed how rare human voice was here; the surfers did not talk, but silently, silently rode the waves.

Since Joseph and Marty were considerate of us, they stopped after two hours, and we took them out for breakfast. We kept asking them how it felt, so that they would not lose language.

"Like a stairwell in an apartment building," said Joseph, which I liked immensely. He hasn't been in very many apartment buildings, so had to reach a bit to get the simile. "I saw somebody I knew coming toward me in the tube, and I shouted, 'Jeff. Hey, Jeff,' and my voice echoed like a stairwell in an apartment building. Jeff and I came straight at each other—mirror tube."

"Are there ever girls out there?" Earll asked.

"There's a few women who come at about eleven," said Marty.

"How old are they?"

"About twenty."

"Why do you cross your heart with water?"

"So the ocean doesn't kill us."

I described the powder-blue tube I had seen. "That part of Sandy's is called Chambers," they said.

I have gotten some surfing magazines, the ones kids steal from the school library, to see if the professionals try to describe the tube. Bradford Baker writes:

> *. . . Round and pregnant in Emptiness*
> *I slide,*
> *Laughing,*
> *into the sun,*
> *into the night.*

Frank Miller calls the surfer

> *. . . mother's fumbling*
> *curly-haired*
> *tubey-laired*
> *son.*

"Ooh, offshores—," writes Reno Abbellira, "where wind and wave most often form that terminal rendezvous of love—when the wave can reveal her deepest longings, her crest caressed, cannily covered to form those peeling concavities we know, perhaps a bit irreverently, as tubes. Here we strive to spend every second—enclosed, encased, sometimes fatefully entombed, and hopefully, gleefully, ejected—Whoosh!"

"An iridescent ride through the entrails of God," says Gary L. Crandall.

I am relieved that the surfers keep asking one another for descriptions. I also find some comfort in the stream of commuter traffic, cars filled with men over twenty, passing Sandy Beach on their way to work.

About the Author

The author at home.
Mānoa Valley, Honolulu (1982).

Maxine Hong Kingston was born in Stockton, California in 1940. She
taught high school in California and Hawai'i for twelve years, and is
now at the University of California, Berkeley. Her first novel, *The
Woman Warrior,* was published in 1976 and received the National
Book Critics Circle Award. *China Men,* published in 1980, received the
National Book Award. She is a Living Treasure of Hawai'i, and won
the Hawai'i Award for Literature in 1983. *Tripmaster Monkey—His
Fake Book* was given the International PEN West Award in Fiction in
1989. In 1998 President Clinton presented her with the National
Humanities Medal.